Prai

"Delightful. . . . The[   ]apstick and satire in this wor

Perhaps the most important, most transcendent, tribute Smelcer offers . . . is not the one he explicitly offers Ted Hughes, but instead the attention paid to Raven's role in Alaskan native culture. In the section titled "In the Language Raven Gave Us," Smelcer claims his place as the only living tribal member who can read and write in his native Ahtna. . . . You've stumbled on the beauty that is John Smelcer's *Raven*."
—*New York Journal of Books*

"The poetry in *Raven* is not just an elder's tale retold; not just another Aesop's, but contemporary and imaginative retelling as a modern fable. And daring, in that a dangerous character is brought to life on pages where love and loss, good and evil co-exist. Smelcer not only colors outside the lines, but he also adds dimensions to the background that will allow readers to delve more deeply into the psychologies of good and evil."
—*Ragazine*

"In a world where such poets are more rare than people might imagine, John Smelcer is one of the truly great poets I have come across in my life. His poetry is genius."
—Ruth Stone, National Book Award winner

"The authenticity of Smelcer's voice . . . makes an electric, multileveled series of parables for our often dark times."—Molly Peacock

RAVEN

Books by John Smelcer

Fiction

Stealing Indians
Savage Mountain
Edge of Nowhere
Lone Wolves
The Trap
The Great Death
Alaskan: Stories from the Great Land

Native Studies

The Raven and the Totem
A Cycle of Myths
In the Shadows of Mountains
The Day That Cries Forever
Durable Breath
Native American Classics
We are the Land, We are the Sea

Poetry

Indian Giver
The Indian Prophet
Songs from an Outcast
Riversong
Without Reservation
Beautiful Words
Tracks
Raven Speaks
Changing Seasons

RAVEN

JOHN SMELCER
Poems

Leapfrog Press
Fredonia, New York

Published in 2019 in the United States by
Leapfrog Press LLC
PO Box 505
Fredonia, NY 14063
www.leapfrogpress.com

Printed in the United States of America

Distributed in the United States by
Consortium Book Sales and Distribution
St. Paul, Minnesota 55114
www.cbsd.com

First Edition

Library of Congress Cataloging-in-Publication Data

Names: Smelcer, John E., 1963- author. | Baskin, Leonard, 1922-2000,
illustrator. | Vienneau, Larry, illustrator. | DeMauro, Don, illustrator.
Title: Raven : poems / John Smelcer ; illustrated by Leonard Baskin,
Larry Vienneau & Don DeMauro.
Description: First edition. | Fredonia, NY : Leapfrog Press LLC, 2019.
Identifiers: LCCN 2018054648 | ISBN 9781948585033 (paperback :
alk. paper)
Subjects: LCSH: American poetry–21st century.
Classification: LCC PS3569.M387 A6 2019 | DDC 811/.54–dc23
LC record available at https://lccn.loc.gov/2018054648

Acknowledgements

Some of the poems in this collection first appeared in the following periodicals:

88: A Journal of Contemporary American Poetry, Anvil & Lyre, Appalachia, Asymptote (Hong Kong), Beloit Poetry Journal, Borderlands: Texas Poetry Review, Chariton Review, Circumference, Common Review, Confluence, Crossborder, Cumberland Poetry Review, Hayden's Ferry Review, International Poetry Review, Kenyon Review, Natural Bridge, North American Review, Pacific Poetry (Vancouver), Pembroke, Prairie Schooner, Ragazine, Rosebud, Runes, Truth and Consequence, Cultural Survival Quarterly, Witness, The Seventh Quarry (UK), Modern Poetry in Translation (UK), Agenda (UK), Bombay Gin, Orbis (UK), Shabdaguchha and *Poetry Ireland Review.*

"After a Sermon at the Church of Infinite Confusion" was a finalist for the *North American Review's* James Hearst Poetry Prize and appeared in *Indian Giver* and *Native American Classics.* "The Birth of Raven" was a finalist for the Marlboro Poetry Prize. "After a Sermon at the Church of Infinite Confusion" and "Returning the Gift" appeared in *Without Reservation* (Truman State UP, 2003). "The Meal" appeared in *Songs from an Outcast* (UCLA, 2000). "Returning the Gift" appeared in *Durable Breath: Contemporary Native American Poetry* (1995). Several poems appeared in *Lost Rivers* and in *Raven Speaks,* a chapbook published by Ted Hughes in 1997. All bilingual poems appeared in *Beautiful Words: The Complete Ahtna Poems* (Truman State UP, 2011). An excerpt appeared in *Plath Profiles* (UK).

The author thanks Ted, Nick, and Frieda Hughes, Carol Orchard Hughes, Emma Cheshire, Bard Young, Catherine Creger, Gary Snyder, David and Helen Constantine, Daniel Weissbort, Valentina Polukhina, Lisa Graziano, Joe Weil, Stanley Kunitz, Ruth and Phoebe Stone, Molly Peacock, Parkman Howe, Aeronwy Thomas, Carole Baldock, Amber Johnson, Abby Letner, Christy Frushour, Larry Vienneau, Don DeMauro, and the estate of Leonard Baskin. This book was supported in part by grants from the Alaska State Council for the Arts, the Alaska Community Foundation, The Elihu Foundation, the Ray and Maxine Stephens Memorial Fund, and Binghamton University's Francis Newman Grant.

Contents

Crow, Raven, and the Hughes-Plath Family Tree

My friendship with Ted Hughes began unexpectedly in the fall of 1997, when I had been invited to England to read at the Poetry Society of London, Tennyson House on the Isle of Wight, and at the Guildford Literary Festival, mostly because several of my poems appeared in  a new collection of Native American poetry published in Guildford. My being from Alaska, many of the poems were about Raven. After the reading, an iron-gray-haired gentleman asked me to join him for a pint at a pub on the other side of the railroad tracks from the Electric Theatre. I have to admit that at the time I didn't know he was the Poet Laureate of England and Sylvia Plath's widower. Needless to say, because free beer was involved I accepted the invitation. Neither Ted nor I could have known the enduring consequences of that encounter and how I would become intricately bound to his legacy and history. With similar interests in poetry, anthropology, and mythology—and both of us keenly interested in the archetypes of the Sacred and the Profane—we had an enjoyable and lively conversation. At some point, we began to co-write a poem about how Raven-Crow created Grendel from *Beowulf,* hoisting Guinness, Old Speckled Hen, and London Pride to our poetic genius. (Photo used with permission of Nicholas Hughes.)

Within weeks, Ted created a limited edition broadside of the poem. Over the next couple of months, we corresponded about *Raven Speaks,* a slender chapbook of my poetry Hughes was to publish from his home in Devon. Ted encouraged me to keep writing Raven poems for a future full-length volume. He asked Leonard Baskin, the artist whose hulking image appeared on the cover of *Crow,* to lend his work to my book. Leonard was enthusiastic about the idea. Ted had been diagnosed with cancer months before we met. He passed away about half a year later from complications.

Seven years later, in 2004, I was again in England, this time studying Shakespeare at Gonville & Caius, one of Cambridge University's ancient colleges (founded in 1342). Almost daily I walked past the house where Ted and Sylvia had once lived. One sunny afternoon, I bought a used copy of Hughes's *Crow* at an open-air market just across from King's College, where dozens of stalls were set up around the cobblestone square— vendors selling everything from T-shirts to jewelry, from bread and pastries to fresh vegetables, local artwork to used books. I think I paid two pounds for it. Re-reading the book in the very place where Ted must surely have written some of the early *Crow* poems, my interest was rekindled in a way that I can only call *consuming*. I felt his bolstering presence as I walked along The Cam and the narrow lanes between colleges and sat on park benches reading his poems aloud. I immediately set out to write the full-length cousin to *Crow*. The poems came out of me as fast as I could write them. I've never experienced such intense poetry writing like it since. I swear, at times I could barely breathe. In one day alone, I wrote four or five of the poems! Over two separate weekends, I worked on poems in Edinburgh, Scotland and in Cardiff, Wales. I wrote several more on the long trans-Atlantic flight home. It took well over a decade to complete the project, but *Raven* is finally ready to take its rightful place alongside its older cousin.

Ted's and Sylvia Plath's son, Nick, lived in Fairbanks, Alaska, where I grew up and attended elementary school, junior and senior high school, and university. He worked at the University of Alaska Fairbanks, where I had been a student throughout the 1980s earning several degrees. At the time, I was living in Anchorage. I introduced myself to Nick as a friend and disciple of his father. Nick and I were the same age. Like me, Nick loved to fish. His father had first brought him to Alaska on a fishing trip when Nick was a teenager. Over two summers, we fished for grayling on the upper Chena River and the Chatanika River, both near Fairbanks. I even took him salmon fishing in Talkeetna. I remember one day while fishing on the Chatanika, I caught a foot-long grayling. Just as

I was about to lift it into the boat, the biggest pike we ever saw in our lives violently snatched the grayling off my line. It must have been four feet long and as thick around as a man's thigh. We spent hours trying to catch that monster, but we never saw it again.

While fishing Clear Creek near my cabin in Talkeetna, Nick caught a salmon while standing on a steep bank. The fish literally yanked  him off the slippery bank and into the icy river. True fisherman as he was, when Nick re-emerged, he still had the salmon hooked. We grilled it for dinner that evening, complemented by a good bottle of wine and a pan of sautéed fiddlehead ferns, which grow abundantly around the cabin in the spring. One winter, we went ice-fishing for burbot on the Tanana River near Fairbanks. (Photo of John Smelcer by Nick Hughes; used with permission.)

During my visits to Fairbanks, Nick would read my Raven poems and give his earnest feedback. Although a marine-and-fisheries biologist by training, I think Nick was happy to be connected to his father's literary life through the book he and I had begun together. More than once, Nick told me that *Crow* was among his favorites of all his father's books. *The Iron Man* was another.

We never really talked about his parents' relationship. To be sure, I don't think Nick had any memories of his mother. He was an infant when she died in 1963. But he did say on numerous occasions that deep down inside he believed he understood his mother's sadness and despair. He didn't worry that it was hereditary or anything like that. If anything, it was his father's death that most affected Nick. During the few times we talked about his parents, Nick complained about all the people who, over the years, had asked him for interviews about his mother or his father. He was wary of anyone who tried to get close to him just to "get the scoop" on his parents. Some people have claimed that Nick moved to Fairbanks—to the northern edge of the world—in an attempt to escape the limelight. But more than anything else, I think Nick moved to Alaska because he loved wilderness and fishing and because he had joyful memories of the time he and his father had visited Alaska.

But increasingly, I noticed a subtle change in Nick. He seemed unhappy and detached. He even quit his job at the university. From about December 2006 until August 2008, I drove up to Fairbanks every few months to cheer him up. We would meet at the Wood Center on campus or at Gulliver's Used Books, both old haunts from my college days. At the time, and in the middle of a devastating depression from a heart-wrenching divorce, I think I needed someone to talk to as well. Our occasional visits heartened us both, if only temporarily.

In the fall of 2008, I moved to upstate New York to complete a Ph.D. in English and creative writing at Binghamton University, where my mentor, John Gardner, had taught up until he died in a motorcycle accident. Before I left, Nick gave me a small box of his fly-fishing flies as a gift. I still have them, too fearful of losing them on a snag to ever use them. We only spoke a few times after that, his tone increasingly despondent. Seven months later, on March 16, 2009, Nick hanged himself in his cabin in the hills above Fairbanks. Like many people close to someone who has taken his or her own life, I sometimes feel that Nick might have lived had I stayed in Alaska. If only I had done *this* or *that*, things might have been different. I felt the same way about my younger brother's suicide in 1988. I felt dreadfully guilty for so long that it was months before I wrote to his sister, Frieda, to tell her how sorry I was and that I too had lost a brother to suicide in a cabin in the hills above Fairbanks.

Time has a way of healing such profound feelings and life does indeed go on for the living. But I'm saddened when I think about how intimately connected my life has been to the losses suffered within the Hughes-Plath family tree. That's why I dedicated this book to Ted and Nick, father and son, my friends.

• • • • •

As a member of an Alaska Native tribe, I have known Raven (*Corvus corax*) all my life as the deified trickster, the ever-selfish, ever-hungry, ever-wicked, ever-present, and always clever god of our Native cultures. I have written several books of Alaska Native mythology. Moreover, as the only tribal member who can read and write fluently in my Native language (Ahtna), I have included a handful of my poems written in Ahtna Athabaskan (the language that Raven gave us) and have rendered them into English, making them among the rarest translations of a language in existence. For a quarter of a century, *Mod-*

ern Poetry in Translation, the journal that Ted Hughes and Daniel Weissbort began back in 1965, has published my poems, including in its 50th anniversary issue.

The Unlikely History of the Art of Raven

The history of the art in *Raven* is worth some comment. When *Crow* was first published by Faber & Faber in 1972, it featured a sketch by Leonard Baskin of a hulking, muscular, and undeniably masculine crow on the cover. Around the same time, Baskin recommended upstate New York artist, Don DeMauro, to receive a Guggenheim Foundation artist fellowship. Baskin and DeMauro had the same New York print agent in Abe Lublin. Based on Baskin's recommendation, Don received the prestigious award. Decades later, around 2010, I met Don at a coffee house

 we both frequented and struck up a friendship, often discussing literature, philosophy, and art and taking lunch together at a pub across the street.

It was during one of those lunches that Don gave permission to use one of his illustrations in this book (p. 122), an illustration of a raven he had made

in the 1970s after seeing Baskin's crow. Although Baskin passed away in 2000, his estate gave permission (Baskin once told Hughes that he wanted his art to be part of this book) to use one of his crow images in the book (p. 120), thereby completing the unlikely circle of relatedness between *Crow* and *Raven*. (Photo by Amber Johnson. Used with permission.)

The illustrations by Larry Vienneau (cover, pp. 28, 39, 47, 49, 53, 56, 59, 63, 108, 117) began as long ago as 1990 for my Alaska Native mythology books *The Raven and the Totem*, *A Cycle of Myths*, and *In the Shadows of Mountains*. Nowadays, Larry is a professor of art at Seminole State University in Florida.

for Nick & Ted

"At the end of forty days, Noah opened the window of
the ark and sent out the raven, which flew to and fro
over the world. When it did not return, Noah sent out
the dove."
—Genesis 8:6

". . . and here comes this black raven,
flapping as if from a great distance, from eternity."
—Hayden Carruth

MYTHOPOETICA

THE BIRTH OF RAVEN

On the Monday after the first week
God accidentally made a black hole
which threatened to destroy Creation.

So He put it in a bag

hammered it with a spiral galaxy
incinerated it in the oven of a thousand suns
and drowned it in every ancient sea.

But when He opened it

Raven flew out from the blackness
blinking and stretching his wicked new wings
bending his unflinching hunger earthward.

RAVENCOLOR

In the beginning
Raven was as white as a glacier

But eon after eon
his wings turned black

      his head
      his feet
      his beak
      his claws

          In the end

his heart became a coal mine
his eyes two black holes
devouring the universe

      atom   by   a t o m

RAVEN'S SONG OF HIMSELF

Raven sang the song of himself

"I am!" he cawed

nothing

"I am!" he shrieked

more nothing

Raven blinked

Caw!

Nothing squared

He blinked again

Caw!

Nothing to infinity

Satisfied, he flew away

the quag of silence lifting his wings

A LINGERING DOUBT

At the end of the tumultuous sixth day
God fashioned Man—a future victim of Raven's

selfishness and greed. Perhaps God said something or
perhaps He said nothing at all. When He was done

God wiped his brow and sighed deeply. It seems
to me that sigh must still be hanging there.

THE DAY AFTER SATURDAY

On the Seventh Day God rested,
exhausted from the busy work-week.

While God dozed, Raven stropped his beak,
turned an eye-pupil toward Creation.

Polar bears slunk into icy dens
wolves slank with tails between their legs
crabs scuttled deeper into the ice-covered sea
caribou stampeded across the tundra
moose sidled behind spruce trees

and maggots squirmed in their rancid flesh-pots.

CREATION MYTH

Raven caught a really nasty flu.

At first his throat scratched
        up scrambled cockroaches.

He gaped
        out swarmed mosquitoes and locusts.

He retched
        out poured typhoid and malaria.

He sneezed
        tsetse flies splattered into existence.

He coughed
        his phlegm became cancer and leprosy.

He crapped
        out sprang cholera and dysentery.

Snot dripping from his beak
        turned into syphilis and gonorrhea.

Eventually, the flu went away
but by then plague and pestilence

had infected the world.

RAVEN AND THE FIRST PEOPLE

from a Haida myth

Raven heard noise from inside a clam.
He bent down and picked it up.

Mankind squatted in the shell,
naked and trembling and starving.

Raven gawked at them, agape.
He peered and peered—

his black eyes blinking,
his twisted mind racing.

Here was what he sought:
someone to call him God.

So he led them out, befriended them,
taught them what they needed to know.

Then he spent forever tormenting them—
they wishing they had never been born.

RAVEN'S THEOLOGY

for Seamus Heaney

People wanted something to believe,

So Raven leaned a stick against a stone
      and the people marveled.

People wanted something to believe,

So Raven stood on one foot holding a white dove
      and the people applauded.

People wanted something to believe,

So Raven placed both black wings over his heart
      and the people wept.

People wanted something to believe,

So Raven tore a struggling hare in half
      and the people prostrated themselves.

Gleeful, Raven flapped away
      laughing at his rubbish heap of lies.

And no one felt cheated,
                no one at all.

WHEN GOD TRIED TO TEACH RAVEN TO SPEAK

Raven perched warily on God's wrist

God held up a puppy

    "Puppy. Say after me, puppy."

Raven gawked and croaked   *Death*

God held up a bunny rabbit

    "Bunny. Can you say bunny?"

Raven guiltily stammered   *Death?*

Frustrated, God held up a naked jabbering man

    "Man. Say man. M-A-N."

Agape, Raven gleefully shouted   *Death!*

God scolded Raven, shaking a finger at him.

Raven snatched it, tore off a piece of God's
index finger and flew away cawing

Death!   *Death!*   *Death!*

Cursing, God went looking for antiseptic and a Band-Aid.

WHEN GOD TRIED TO TEACH RAVEN MATHEMATICS

God held up a blathering naked man,
his limbs thrashing, his eyes bulging.

Then he held up one in his other hand.

    "One plus one equals two," He said

in his best instructional voice. Raven seized one
by its slapeskin neck, popped its head off
with his thumb like a dandelion.

    "Two minus one equals one!" he squealed,

cheerfully beginning to understand the concept.

    "Math is fun! Let's do it again!"

Horrified, God skipped the lesson on division.

WHEN GOD TRIED TO TEACH RAVEN COMPASSION

God tried to teach Raven compassion.

He sat on a stool of mountain
holding a nervous cat in his lap.

"Pet the pretty kitty," He said.

But Raven snatched it,
dashed its brains against a cliff,

      and ate it.

God never tried to teach him again.

RAVEN REMEMBERS (TO THE WORLD'S DISMAY)

And it came to pass in those days
that Raven got amnesia;

    he simply couldn't remember his name.

Everyone told him it was

    Love or *Kindness* or *Joy.*

But those words stuck in his craw
like maggots struggling from disaster to disaster—

    No, wait! It *was* Disaster!

WHAT RAVEN HAD FOR BREAKFAST

A long time ago
Raven decided to be a mother
so she laid a giant egg—
as big and white as a beluga whale.

From her nest-perch of felled redwoods
she saw God sitting on his own two eggs,
watched them hatch, spilling their slime-naked
beings into the world, watched them grow,
dishonor their father, multiply,
witnessed the one murder the other.

Appalled, Raven fried her egg
sunny-side up in a pan with butter.

THE TEMPTATION OF EVE

One day while God was away stirring galaxies

Raven was flying around
when he saw a magnificent Garden.
In the middle stood a great tree
surrounded by yellow police tape
                        and neon signs flashing:

Forbidden!   Forbidden!   Forbidden!

Raven had a cunning idea.

When he saw the woman coming
Raven set up a stand with his own sign:

        "Apples! 5 Cents Each!"

And the snake—the snake—
that slithering ruiner

just laughed

                & laughed.

THE MARK OF CAIN

Raven saw the whole damned thing:

brother slaying brother
a mother's sorrow
a father's grief
God's bewilderment

     and His proclamation of exile.

Raven strode up to Cain
throttled him
pecked a gash on his

     treacherous face—

infuriated that some hack
dared impersonate his

     splendid malevolence.

GOD APOLOGIZES FOR THE FLOOD
(RAVEN SEIZES AN OPPORTUNITY)

Raven was eavesdropping
the day God broke up with humanity.

"It's not you, it's me," said God
trying to soften the imminent blow,

while waving a conjuring hand
to summon the darkening tempests.

Ever the price-gouger, Raven sold
life-preservers at ten times the going rate.

RAVEN FLY TRAP

Raven was bored silly,
so he invented a fun new game.

He'd hide in a bush crying,

      "Help!"   "Help!"

Whenever someone came he'd jump up
and bash their brains out with a club.

Eventually, he tired of the game and flapped away
looking for someone else to torment.

And wouldn't you know it, there was good old Job

      just as happy as can be.

EXODUS RAVEN

For forty years
after leaving Egypt,
Moses led his people
through the desert.

Every time they found a likely place
to settle, Raven made a sign
and posted it for everyone to see:

    "NO LOITERING!"

Moses took it as an omen from God
and begrudgingly moved along;
his mounting discontent a burning bush.

THE OTHER TEMPTATION OF CHRIST

Raven spied Jesus wandering in the desert.

He tried to tempt Christ with

        lust and fornication—

    two sweet-mouthed whores under a black wing.

He tried to corrupt Christ with

        iniquity and greed—

    wine flagons and Rolex knock-offs under the other.

Through it all Jesus—sweet Jesus—smiled

        forgiving and forgiving.

Confounded, Raven flew away
and whispered in the ear of Judas Iscariot.

Amen.   Amen.

PASSOVER, 33 A.D.

Raven stood on a cobbled street in Jerusalem

      disguised as a leper,

his black wings tucked beneath a robe,
listening to Pontius Pilate
plead if he should free Jesus
or a known thief and murderer.

Slyly, with a mischievous glint in his eye,
Raven began to shriek,

      "Free Barabbas! Free Barabbas!"

Before long the hissing crowd
was shouting and doing the wave

while Pontius Pilate—utterly confused—

      wrung his sweaty palms.

GOLGOTHA

Early Christian tradition relates this story

After inciting the heckling mob
to free Barabbas instead of Jesus
Raven flew up to Golgotha
and awaited the ghastly procession up Via Dolorosa.

He witnessed the ensuing spectacle in horror,

      holding his wings over his ears
when they hammered nails through Christ's hands,

      holding his wings over his eyes
when they drove a spike through Christ's feet.

For a long time he listened to the taunts
of the one criminal, his insane laughter.

No longer amused, Raven pecked his eyes out.

THE SUBSTITUTE

Satan needed to go on vacation.

(Apparently it's really stressful being evil all the time.)

So he thought and thought
who could be his replacement—

who was twisted and warped enough to pull it off?

And then he spied Raven
cheating a rosy-cheeked child out of her ice cream cone.

BEOWRAVEN

co-written with Ted Hughes in Guildford, 1997

Raven wanted a pet

so he slogged into a fen
fashioned a fanglorious beast

    from filth and slime and muck

named it Grendel
stropped its wicked claws and teeth
stroked its mudruckled fur

then pointed at Hrothgar's unwary keep
commanded

    "Fetch!"

& the gorged and grisly creature
always returned

    with a heap of bones

RAVEN'S VISION

One day after Raven ate a pod of walrus
he was flying around when he saw something
wiggling on a beach. He had never seen
such a furless creature, so he asked its name
and it croaked out Man, crapped itself,
and retched on Raven's wing. Raven grabbed
the naked, gaping thing to shake it, but
in that instant he had a vision so terrible
he dropped it in its feces and flew away
cursing as he went.

In that lifeless touch he saw

> plagues, religion, corruption
> Hamlet, Othello, and Lear
> Facism and genocide
> saw two cities extinguished in a flash
> saw a heaving seatide of humanity
> a world buried in filth
> the seas aswirl with flotsam
> saw an old Indian crying on tv
> an oily desert afire
> email, spam, and Wall Street
> two great towers crumbling
> and the eventual death
> of every other living thing.

If Raven had been thinking that day
he'd have taken up a rock,
smashed the shit out of it, and eaten it.

RAVEN SENDS OUT
A SEARCH PARTY

Raven wanted to find God
so she made Man from a dung heap
and sent him into the world.

"Where is God?"

Man ripped apart the earth
to find him, sent machines
into the dark void, toppled
every tree in case
he were nestled in the roots,
ploughed every field in case
he were an unturned stone.

"Where is God?"

He dissected cats and dogs and toads
to look inside their smooth guts
as if God was lodged in the liver,
tortured his own kind who did not know
and killed those who might.

"Where is God?" they cried, gnashing their teeth.

"Where is God?" they prayed, kneeling on thick wallets.

"We need his compassion!"

RAVEN'S HIT LIST

Raven was tired of competing
with other make-believe beings;

there simply wasn't enough imagination to go around.

So he stole a pre-molar from a child
and hid it under his pillow—

Fairy-bait for the Tooth Fairy.

That night when she flew into the room—
her tiny insectine wings abuzz—

he wacked her with a fly swat
and spread her on his toast like jelly.

After breakfast,
Raven went out looking for the Easter Bunny

with a shotgun.

RAVEN REMODELS THE WORLD

As told to me by elders on the Kuskokwim and Yukon Rivers

A very long time ago, Raven was tired of the world
he had created, so he destroyed it in a flood.

But first he built a giant raft
upon which he placed a male and female
of every species:

> two moose, caribou, musk ox,
> polar bear and grizzly bear,
> black-tailed deer, red fox and arctic fox,
> lynx, wolverine, and beaver—
>
> he had them all.

Eventually, the water subsided, Raven
released the animals, and the world was anew.

What? You've already heard this one before?

EXTINCTION THEORY

Raven, Unicorn, and Grizzly Bear
were talking when an argument broke out.

Naturally, Raven started the whole thing.

Mad as hell, Grizzly chased them both.

When the bear closed in, Raven tripped Unicorn
and escaped while Grizzly was busy feasting.

RAVEN AND KILLER WHALE

Raven flew around the world looking for something to eat
when he saw Killer Whale swimming in a bay.

He gathered a bundle of sticks and flew down to the whale.
"I am your cousin," he said, thinking of all that oily meat.

"Ridiculous!" replied Whale.
"I am of the sea. You are of the sky."

But Raven was cunning. He thought up a great lie.
"The inside of our mouths are the same," he said.

As soon as Killer Whale opened his mouth
Raven ran straight into his belly and built a fire.

For months, Raven ate that whale from the inside out.
All the while, Whale begged and pleaded for mercy.

Haven't you learned by now there are no happy endings?

THE DOG HUSBAND

from a Haida myth

Maybe I shouldn't tell this story, but one time
Raven was actually nice. I know. Go figure.

A long time ago there was this young woman
who had a pet dog that fell in love with her.

One day he turns himself into a man and marries the woman,
who gives birth to three puppies. The villagers kill the husband

and exile the poor mother. Raven sees the miserable
and starving family, takes pity on their plight.

So he befriends them, teaches them how to hunt and fish,
how to make shelter and fire, which plants they can eat.

Years later the mother hears her children laughing in the
sweat house.
She peers in and sees their dog skins

hanging by the door. *They're actually humans!*
She runs in and tosses their skins on the fire

so they can never become dogs again. Years later, as young men,
they save their old village during a famine and become chiefs.

There's no accounting for Raven's uncharacteristic generosity in
this story.

WHEN RAVEN TRIED BENEVOLENCE

Raven wanted to be a kinder god
so she gave mankind a bouquet of flowers,
which turned out to be poisonous.

She tried to fashion for them butterflies,
but they turned into a locust horde.

She tried to slake a wicked drought,
but flooded the world by mistake.

Terrified of future gifts,
mankind begged Raven
to stop trying to be so nice.

RAVEN, THE PROBLEM SOLVER

If you cut a salmon's head right down the middle
you will see two gray stones, one in each hemisphere

In the beginning, salmon could only swim on the surface
where hungry bears and eagles could easily catch them.

Chief-of-the-Salmon People pleaded,

"Help us, Great Raven!"

That smart Raven placed two small stones
inside each salmon's head, weighting them down.

Since then, salmon can swim in deep water
and bears and eagles have to work for their supper.

THE CORPSE KING

Once there was an Eskimo village
at the base of a steep cliff. But one

winter after a blizzard, an overhang
formed above the village. Ever-hungry,

Raven stomped on it until an avalanche
buried everyone. For the rest of winter

and all spring, Raven dined on people,
plucking out eyeballs like blueberries—

a delicacy. When Kajortok, the white fox,
asked why he did it, Raven convulsed,

gaped, hacked up a finger, and burped,
"Because and because and because . . ."

RAVEN'S MASK

Raven carved an eagle mask. When he put it on
he turned into an eagle. He flew to a nearby village.

When the people saw him they said,
"Look at the powerful eagle, so wise and strong."

So they became the Eagle Clan. For the first time
Raven felt loved. But one day he lost his mask.

When he returned to the village
the people threw stones and yelled at him,

"Go away, Raven. You're bad luck.
You'll frighten away our beautiful eagle."

THE BLUE PRINCE

Raven saw Hamlet crying at his father's funeral.

The king really died of syphilis
he contracted from a chambermaid,

but Raven wanted to have some fun
so he pretended to be the dead king's ghost.

He told Hamlet that he was murdered in a garden
by his poisonous brother who was banging his mother.

From the grand lie Elsinore
became a cordoned crime scene—

fly-swarming corpses and chalk outlines everywhere,
the whole damn place come undone.

THE BIRTH OF IAGO

Shakespeare had writer's block in 1603.

He just couldn't create a despicable enough villain for his new play.

So he went to The Slaughtered Lamb for a few pints and darts
where he met Raven just returned from bringing in The Plague.

Ever the remorseless deceiver,

Raven lied, cheated & pinched Willy's money purse;
and he did it all with a straight face while saying,

"Honesty is the best policy!" &
"*This* is a face you can trust!"

With eyes aglint,

Willy ran home and crafted lying Iago from his inkwell,
his soul an abyss as black as Raven's craw.

INSTIGATOR

In 1692, Raven flew to Salem, Massachusetts for a crack,
but he quickly became bored with the Puritans

      who simply didn't know how to have any fun.

But then he spied two girls sticking out their tongues at an old lady
who chastised them for picking their snot in public.

Disguised as a black-frocked vicar
Raven whispered, "She's a witch"
and suddenly both girls went into epileptic fits.

As the good townspeople gathered around
Raven began to sing a contagious song:

      "Ding, dong the witch is dead!"

In no time, a hundred accusing fingers were pointing like
pistols.

FRANKENRAVEN

"Remember that I am thy creature. Misery made me a fiend. Love me, and I shall again be virtuous.
—The Monster to Frankenstein

Horror-struck by his hideous creation
Raven flew away cawing, *"Ugly! Ugly! Ugly!"*

For the rest of his needy days,
Man searched in vain for a father-figure
to love him, put a steadfast hand on his shoulder,
teach him how to handle a jackknife
and play catch on the lawn—

striving to find any god upon which to put a face.

STOOL PIGEON

Raven gawked as Custer and his soldiers
came over the hill at Little Big Horn,

thinking it might be a good place for a *Starbucks.*

While George was busy combing his golden mustache
Raven flew down to warn Crazy Horse and Sitting Bull.

He jabbered and remonstrated,
pointed a feathery finger toward the hill;
preening himself like a sissy,
playing a kind of proto-charade

Shortly thereafter, almost two thousand Indians
turned the green, rolling hills into a killing field.

TO BUILD A FIRE

after a story by Jack London

One day in the sixty-below Yukon
Raven saw a man stumbling in the snow.

While he watched the man struggling
to build a fire beneath a tree

      Raven poured himself a cup of coffee,
      ate blueberry scones and biscotti.

And when at last he saw a tinderwisp of smoke

      Raven stomped and stomped
      until boughsnow avalanched
      and smothered the flames,

extinguishing the dumbstruck miner

waiting for the coldsnap of frost

      to ease into his bones.

RAVEN & VINNY

One starry night in France, Raven spied Vincent Van Gogh
gazing out a window at the asylum in Saint-Rémy-de-Provence.

Raven wriggled through the steel bars,
perched on the easel while the artist toiled.

"What's that supposed to be?" "Looks like a child did it."
"You're crazy! No one's ever going to buy that!"

All night and the next day Raven taunted Vincent
wherever he went, even to the loo.

"Mark my words: You'll never amount to anything."
"No one will ever remember your name."

Despite it all, Vincent kept on painting:
his paintbrush in one hand, covering one ear with the other.

When he couldn't stand another minute,
                                    Vincent cut off the other ear.

RAVEN CUM LAUDE

Ever-studious,

Raven went to Cambridge

to study religion and philosophy;

but he left mid-semester

   realizing

it was all about him anyhow.

RAVEN'S TITANIC FUN

April 15, 1912

Raven flapping across the North Atlantic
on his way to visit cousins at the Tower of London.

Through the starry night he spies
the *Titanic*, New York bound, icebergs dead ahead.

     On a lark, he lands,
hides in the wheelhouse and waits
until the captain leaves the helm
then, in his best impersonation,
calls down to the engine room,

    "Full Speed Ahead!"

Satisfied with his mayhem
Raven resumes his flight,
humming some tune he heard
a trio playing as the ship

     plunged
        into
            the   abyss

as deep and dark as Raven's gullet.

HEIL RAVEN

One of Hitler's henchmen
had a parrot that would squawk,

"Himmel! Leiber ein Wiener Schnitzel!"
Not to be outdone,
Hitler bought a talking raven.

But despite his best efforts
all it ever said was

      "Blitzkrieg! Blitzkrieg!"

      Ga-gok! Ga-gok!

which was Raven's way of laughing.

Little by little, the word became
all that Hitler could mutter.

He spraddled up to his Field Marshalls shrieking,

      "Blitzkrieg! Blitzkieg!"

And the war-weary nations readied their graves.

RAVENS AT AUSCHWITZ

"The number of ravens increased considerably
and everybody knew why."
—Primo Levi, *Survival at Auschwitz*

In January, after the Nazis marched 20,000 prisoners
from Auschwitz before the advance of the Allies
only the sick and dying remained in the camp hospital
called Ka-Be.

For ten days the sick waited in their own filth,
stacking corpses like cordwood in the cold,

                             their constant companions

distended bellies as empty as their hope—
and murders of ravens feasting on the dead.

ROLE MODEL

August 6-9, 1945

Overjoyed, Raven watched as one nation
dropped atomic bombs on another

vaporizing cities in clouds of corpse-dust.

Visibly moved, tears welled in Raven's eyes,
black as atomic shadows seared into sidewalks.

"Good, my children," he croaked.
"I have taught you well."

CIVIL DISOBEDIENCE

December 1, 1955.
Raven catches a bus in Montgomery, Alabama.

Seeing that he's black and all,
the driver tells Raven to sit in the colored section
with the rest of his kind.

At the next stop, some white passenger
tells this young black woman sitting across from Raven
to give up her seat 'cause the white section's full.

Sick and tired of this segregation crap, Raven goads her:

>   Don't move an inch.
>   You paid for that seat.
>   Don't give 'em the satisfaction.
>   They ain't no better than you.

After the shit hits the fan, Raven marches away,
veering his cunning eye toward Selma.

ELECTRIC RAVEN (DYLAN PLUGS IN)

Six months before the 1965 Newport Folk Festival
where concertgoers booed Dylan for going electric.

Raven ogles Bob Dylan tuning his acoustic guitar.

He sidles up & hands him
a shiny new electric guitar.

"You got to get with the times
                    like a rolling stone
or you'll gather moss,
            be a complete unknown,"
jabbered Raven,

while a mumbling Dylan scribbled lines to a song.

NEW YORK CITY, 1969

John Lennon and Yoko Ono
invite Raven to an anti-war protest.

He mused at the long-haired hippies
in bell-bottoms and tie-dyed shirts
chanting and waving hastily-painted signs.

"Make Love, Not War!"

That night, as the protestors free-loved
in Flower-Power vans with Mary Jane smoke
billowing from open windows,
Raven craftily reversed the order of their signs.

The next day,
a leering Richard Nixon joined them in their march.

RAVEN'S DOPPELGANGER

Raven wanted to see the Southwest

    so he bought sunglasses and a Nikon,
    flip-flops and Bermuda shorts,
    took a Greyhound bus to the Grand Canyon
    where he met Coyote
    selling souvenirs on a roadside.

"You look just like me," said Raven.

"No, you look like me," replied Coyote.

It really was like looking in a mirror, only different.

The tricksters came up with a mischievous plan.

    Coyote yelped in delight
    Raven rubbed his wings together

their wicked plan as cunning as a leaning shithouse.

PHARMA RAVEN

Raven wanted to be a zillionaire
so he started a pharmaceutical company that manufactured
pills for a disease that didn't exist before. He invented
a scary disorder name & trademarked it, charged an arm & a leg
& tempted doctors with huge kickbacks. Then he blew a wad
of cash buying ad space in slick magazines to convince people
they had his phony disease:

Do you sometimes have to pee in the middle of the night?
Do you occasionally have a little trouble falling asleep?
Do you feel bloated or gassy after eating an enormous meal?
Do you infrequently suffer from mild headaches or dandruff?
These are all symptoms you may have a debilitating disease.

In teeny tiny font he listed all the potential side effects, which
included: bleeding eye balls, liver failure, loss of hair and teeth,
brain lesions, erectile dysfunction, anal leakage, explosive diarrhea
accompanied by uncontrollable flatulence, partial facial paralysis,
gangrene of the genitals, and in rare cases, death.

Afterward, a gloating Raven in a Speedo
did cannonballs in his giant vault of money.

RAVEN'S SHELL GAME

Raven set up at the corner of 42nd and Broadway.

He placed three shells on a table and shouted,

    "Step right up! Everyone's a winner!"

Christ, Buddha, and Mohammad, who were on vacation,
stopped to watch and listen, wearing mirrored sunglasses,
sandals with white socks, and T-shirts that said "I ♥ New York."

Raven pegged them for pigeons right away.

    "Guess which shell the pea is under and you're a winner!"

All three prophets put down a twenty.

Seemingly, Raven placed a pea under one shell,
but it was really a slight of hand, then he shuffled them saying,

    "The wing is faster than the eye."

Christ raised a shell and there was a pea!

    Raven was bewildered.

Then Buddha lifted a shell and there was a pea under it as well.

Astonished, Raven couldn't believe his eyes!

Finally, Mohammad picked up the remaining shell, and miraculously also found a pea.

Beaten at his own game, Raven flew away in a fit, squawking,

"Cheats! Cheats! Cheats!"

FREUD DISCOVERS THE GOD COMPLEX

Scene:

Raven prostrate on a plush, red sofa in an office somewhere in Vienna. The room is well appointed with fine Victorian furniture. Dr. Freud, in a grey suit, sits in a wingback chair examining his notes after an hour of listening to Raven talk about how he created the world and everything in it and how he influenced history at crucial moments.

Freud (looking up from his notes; a hand on his chin):

> So, you believe that you are God?
> Very interesting.
> Now tell me about your mother.

RAVEN GOES ON A GAME SHOW

"For a new 60 inch curved ultra-high-definition TV,"
declares the Ken Doll host who just boinked Barbie in his
dressing room,
"What is the square root of 998,001?"
"That's easy," replies Raven without blinking. "999."

"Correct!" says the host checking his looks in a mirror.
"For an all-expenses-paid Caribbean cruise vacation,
what is the Latin taxonomic name for polar bear?"
With a gleeful knowing smirk Raven replies,
"*Ursus maritimus.* Come on, give me a hard one."

"Right again!" announces the cleft chinned host.
"Finally, for a brand new red convertible sports car,
 how do you spell *Love?*" In a hissy fit caught on camera,
Raven smashes the set and flies away.

GENDER BENDER

In all the stories
Raven was sometimes ♂
and sometimes ♀

He just couldn't make up her mind what she was.

On the one hand
She loved airing out his junk
beneath a miniskirt;
but *hotdamn* he looked good in a tux & tie.

Gender-befuddled,
Raven once stood outside
the men's & women's toilets
at a KFC for half an hour
trying to decide which one to use.

RAVEN PULLS HIS TRUMP CARD

While buying a bag of bagels in Manhattan
Raven saw this $\mathbf{BIGLY}$ name on the front of a skyscraper.

What arrogance! thought Raven. *What a big baller!*
This huckster reminds me of me!

So he put on an orange-faced-yellow-haired Halloween mask

      and he lied & lied,
      mocked & demeaned everyone who opposed him
      like an eighth grade bully,

crowed that he was the most smartest jeanyes he ever knew
& promised America he'd wreck the world

if only the people would make him king.

              And wouldn't you know they did.

RAVEN WRITES THE EPITAPH FOR HUMANITY & TAKES OUT A 'FOR SALE' AD

Billions suffered & perished,
but a few got rich along the way.

(They all died too, but what the hay!)

Requiesce in pace

FOR SALE!

One busted planet. High miles.
Rust-bucket. Leaks oil.
Restoration project or part out.
As is. No warranty. Make offer.
Will consider trades.

THE LAW OF ENTROPY

At the end of Time
the sun expanded
engulfing the inner planets
charring them to clinkers.

      At the last moment
Raven escaped into the vacuum,

the last living thing on earth:

         nothing left to eat
         nothing left to steal
         nothing left to torment.

Everything scorched. Everything burned;

the inglorious demise of one little Creation.

Directly, the blackness of the universe
absorbed the blackness of Raven—

   nothing   to   n o t h i n g.

IN THE LANGUAGE RAVEN GAVE US

ZEN RAVEN

Raven wanted to learn patience.

So he sat amid stones
on a mountain
for a thousand years—

neither he nor the stones
saying a word.

SAGHANI GGAAY ZEN

Saghani Ggaay den ghaetl'.

Xa' dii daa yae' ts'es
dghelaay ts'en'
c'etiy xay—

Saghani Ggaay 'eł ts'es
kole ghaas.

THE MEANING OF LIFE

Lynx asked Raven the meaning of life.

Raven pondered and pondered,
starved himself for a week.

Finally, he bent over double
heaved and heaved, spat out

       Selfishness and *Cruelty*

vomited the slick black bile of

       Suffering.

C'EYIITS' GHANII

Niduuyi dzak' Saghani Ggaay c'eyiits' ghanii.

Saghani Ggaay ninic'ezet 'eł ninic'ezet,
tsen szełghaen dzaen konst'aghi.

Gaxan, Saghani Ggaay zok
koy 'eł koy, tuh

Ninidedzet 'eł *c'ahwdi'aadze'*

koy ket' t'uuts' c'ezitu'

Tanizii.

PRAYER SINGER

A dead raven along the river's edge.

I make a small fire on a sandbar
sing an old Indian prayer
and the universe will understand.

YII NAHWGHI'AAN

Saghani k'ez laak 'Atna'tu.

Sii idiłk'aan saas tabaaghe
Sii yii nahwghi'aan
'eł ne'eł dakozet uk'eani'dizet.

A MINOR CORRECTION

Back when Raven was a person in mythic times
all rivers ran both ways:

      upriver and downriver.

Raven decided that life was too easy for people,
so he made rivers flow only one way.

All the following days were toil.

CU'TS'ENDZE' GGAAY

Saghani Ggaay 'eł koht'aene ghile' yenida'a
'eł 'Atna'tu len nadaeggi xuyae':

nae' 'eł daa'.

Saghani Ggaay yaa naa tae gha denaey,
xa' yen tsii 'Atna'tu len yaen' ts'iłghu.

Dzaenta 'udii ukesdez'taet yihk'ets'en.

HUNTER'S LUCK

In Ahtna Athabaskan society, it is said,
women were not permitted to hunt with
men because they brought bad luck.

Once, I was hunting caribou beside a lake
near a mountain west of Tazlina Glacier.

The morning was overcast,
rain dripped from clouds.

Suddenly, a white raven
landed on a dark-colored rock.

That raven turned herself
into a beautiful woman.

We ate blueberries and crowberries
while making love, and

while I was resting and watching
fish jump out of the water

to eat mosquitoes, she flew away
toward the mountains

singing a love song—
caw, caw, caw.

CANAANI

"Hunter's Luck" in Ahtna

Tl'ahwdinaesi.

Yaak'e kuztset sacaan,
caan natadghitaan k'os.

Gaxan, saghani ggaay
nangit'ak katnalkaadzi.

Saghani ggaay cic'uunen
nay'sdeltsiin kasuundze' ts'akae.

Gigi gheli 'aan 'eł giznae
ighil'aen', 'eł

hwnaexghesdan 'eł yiits
kay' dalt'ak

kuggaedi, saghani yen t'ak
ts'en' dghelaay

kay'ghilgaac—
ggaek gok, ggaek gok, ggaek gok.

WHEN RAVEN WAS KILLED

My full-blood Indian grandmother told me this story,
the only one I know in which Raven dies.

When Raven had lived for a very long time
Ahtna warriors killed him
put him in a gunny sack
carried him up a mountain
and dropped the sack over a cliff.

But Raven came back to life.
He went down the mountain
and killed them all.

SAGHANI GGAAY DYILAAK

Saghani Ggaay c'a tiy dadenelnende
'Atna hwt'aene yen dyilaak
cuut yen 'ałcesi stl'uuni
łuyinintaan yen dghelaay
'ałcesi naghilghaets k'aats'.

Saghani Ggaay uyiits' dez'aan.
Cetaniyaa 'eł utl'ahwdghelnen.

PLAYING HIDE-AND-SEEK
WITH RAVEN

While Porcupine counted to ten
Raven hid behind a spruce tree
and turned himself into a cow caribou.

Poor Porcupine never figured it out.

NIŁCA' STANA'STNEŁ'IISI
KAE SAGHANI GGAAY

Nuuni taak k'e hwlazaan
Saghani Ggaay koł'ii niidze ts'abaeli
'eł cic'uunen udzih yats'iidi.

Nuuni tege 'sdade'estniige.

RAVEN AND THE BUTTERFLY

Raven watched a caterpillar crawling on a branch.
It made itself into a cocoon and transformed

into a beautiful butterfly.

Raven was jealous for six months.

SAGHANI GGAAY 'EŁ LAHTS'IBAAY

Saghani Ggaay gguux dzuuts'i 'aen uus zucene'.
Gguux dzuuts'i ggux hwnax tsii 'eł zdlaen

kasuundze' lahts'ibaay.

Saghani Ggaay lae ts'ae gistaani na'aay.

CORVUS CORAX

AFTER A SERMON AT THE
CHURCH OF INFINITE CONFUSION

At ten, Mary Caught-in-Between
came home from sunday school,
told every animal and bird and fish
they couldn't talk anymore,
told her drum it couldn't sing anymore,
told her feet they couldn't dance anymore,
told her words they weren't words anymore,
told raven he wasn't a god anymore,
said god was a starving white man
with long hair and blue eyes and a beard
who no one loved enough to save
when they nailed him to a totem pole.

PARADISE LOST

I feel bad for ravens. Really.
God used to get more respect.

But in the cities nowadays they have become

> beggars & pick-pockets
> alcoholics & vagabonds
> road-kill scavengers
> & dumpster-divers
> squawking over leftovers
> pushing grocery carts
> up and down the streets.

In storefronts and alleyways cops admonishing vagrants,

> "Move along!"

At every intersection a wretched bird with a sign,

> "WILL WERK 4 FUDE!"

On every street corner a raven rattling a tin cup—

the distance between heaven and hell

> thin as a dime.

UNEMPLOYMENT LINE

Yesterday, I stood in the unemployment line
all day with Raven and Coyote,
Turtle and two out-of-work Kachinas.

Seems there's no jobs for Indian poets or gods.

RAVEN TAKES A CAREER

Raven wanted to be a writer
so he starved himself for a week
flogged himself with a baseball bat
learned how to do without sleep
practiced begging for recognition
pretending he was visible to the world.

"See me!

                    he shouted from a tree.

"See me!"

      Caw!   Caw!

Then he curled up and cried himself to sleep.

AMERICAN INDIAN LITERATURE POLICE REJECT RAVEN

Raven sent his poems to an anthology
of American Indian literature;
and although he created the world
and everything in it,
all his poems were rejected.

Other Indians

said his eyes weren't dark enough,
said his feathers weren't black enough.

Dejected, Raven flew over mountains,
alighted on a branch, and cawed
his lonely name into the night

trying to assure himself that he still existed.

RETURNING THE GIFT

All summer, I have been feeding a raven
who comes to the river asking for salmon.

For weeks, we talk of the origin of things
while I cut fish to dry in the sun.

Months later, when geese fly overhead
in long, slow arrows, I am lost moose hunting.

When night falls upon its dark knees and the moon
is a fingernail at the rim of the world,

I listen to tight-stringed wind
from inside my fluttering tent, and by morning,

in a shudder, the world is wintered.
Quietly, through the gray wolf of the north

I watch the raven arrive to lead me from the forest,
tree by tree, until I am home and we speak for the last
time.

Tsin'aen, Saghani Ggaay. Tsin'aen.
"Thank you, Great Raven. Thank you."

As he flies toward far ochre mountains,
I can hear him singing and singing.

THE MEAL

It is evening and Denali is close
on the blue-edged horizon.

A jay watches me from atop a ski
sticking upright from the crusted snow

outside the cabin door, his careful eyes noting
where crumbs fall from the warm bread in my hand.

From above a scraggly forest
of black spruce and muskeg

a raven arrives quietly to perch
across the clear cut. I do not know

if his dark eyes watch me or the crumbs
lying on the snow. I return to the wood stove,

and looking out the window see the jay
stealing his meal, and the raven

drifting low over frozen marsh,
disappearing into darkening trees.

KINSHIP

Last night, I dreamed
against the trunk of a great tree
full of ravens. In the vision,
I joined them fighting for the flesh
of spawned salmon and flying high
above our small village
sprawled along the braided river's edge.

In the revealing light of dawn, I awoke
naked and curled beneath the leafless tree,
a dozen of the black birds around me,
their patient eyes unflinching.

The closest cocked his head and cawed,
and though I cried, "Speak, Brother Raven, Speak,"

my voice only shooed him away.

WITNESS

I discover a wolf's chewed-off paw
wedged in a trap, the close snow trampled

in gore. But what amazes me most
are raven tracks at the edge of the chain's

length. I can't help but wonder was the raven
there to pity the wolf? To encourage him?

To recite last rites? Or was he simply
awaiting an easy meal? And did the wolf

gnaw faster trying to escape
the lesser of two evils?

RAVEN ORACLE

One wintry day I came upon Raven sitting on a low branch.
"Wise Raven, why is snow cold?" I asked.
The black bird stared at me, dumbfounded.
I thought up another question:
"Brother Raven, why do trees sway in the wind?"
The black bird looked around as if searching for a hidden camera.
Growing weary of the silence, I asked one last question:
"Can't you understand what I'm saying?"

Receiving no reply, I left irritated.

Soon afterward Lynx came up to Raven.
"Why didn't you answer that man's questions?" he asked.
"He asked such idiotic questions," replied Raven,
"that I treated him like an idiot."

A RAVEN FUNERAL

In the white hills above my cabin
I come upon a hundred ravens—

little black-robed priests—circling a small field,
sitting in trees cawing at the center

where a raven lies dead in the snow. As if
by signal, they stop and fly away,

leaving an uninvited guest
standing in the silence of their wake.

THE GREAT RELIGIOUS
TRIAL COMES TO AN END

Shortly after missionaries
came into the country

a jury of Indians put Raven on trial,
demanding he prove he was a god.

Raven pointed to the mountains,
to the lakes and rivers and seas.

   "I made these for you," he said.

He pointed a wingfinger to the sun,
the moon, and the stars.

   "I stole these for you," he said.

He named all the creatures,
great and small, timid and bold.

   I fashioned these for you," he said.

In the end, Indians voted unanimously,
sentencing Raven to obscurity.

A MODERN DAY
INDIAN FAIRY TALE

Raven and Coyote made a bet
who could create the tallest

mountain. For forty days
they sang and danced

used all their magic
and every powerful word

and song they knew. In the end,
all they made was a field of trampled

grass. They couldn't make a single hill
because Indians don't believe in them anymore.

RAVEN ADDRESSES THE JURY
AFTER BEING PRONOUNCED
GUILTY AS THE ARCHITECT
OF ALL HUMAN SUFFERING

I did it and I meant to do it!

        I'd do it all over again!

Spreading strife is my greatest joy,
for discord is the creator of all great things.

        Triumph is born from tribulation.

        You'd be nothing without me!

Wherever there is Time there is Sorrow.
Wherever there is Sorrow

        you'll find me gloating.

ROADKILL

I killed God with my pickup truck.

He was guzzling roadkill when I came speeding along.
At the last minute, he reluctantly abandoned his meal,

flew up the wrong way, smashed into my windshield,
lay in a feathery crumple on the highway,

feet up. I stopped, got out to look, cringing,
eyes darting, waiting for some bad shit to happen—

like a scared rabbit cowering in an open field.

THE MYTH-MAKERS IMBIBE

for Ted

Raven and Ted Hughes walk into a pub
and each orders a pint of Guinness.

"So, what did you think of my book?" asks Hughes.
"Lies!" says Raven. "I never did any of those things."

"Like hell!" exclaims Hughes.
"God save the Queen!" burps Raven.

"Bloody American!" yells Hughes.
"Bloody Brit!" shouts Raven.

"I love you, bloke," says Raven.
"Right back at you, stupid git," says Hughes.

Raven laughs hysterically.
Hughes falls to the floor.

And after the seventh round
the waiter stops bringing drinks.

ABOUT THE AUTHOR

John Smelcer is a member of the Traditional Native Village of Tazlina and a shareholder of Ahtna Native Corporation. For three years, he was the executive director of the Ahtna Heritage Foundation, charged with preserving Ahtna culture, history, and language. Taught by every living elder in his tribe, John is one of the last speakers of his severely endangered language and the only tribal member able to read and write fluently in it. In 1998, he published *The Ahtna Noun Dictionary and Pronunciation Guide.* He is also one among the last speakers of Alutiiq, a neighboring, yet unrelated language. In 2010, he edited and published a noun dictionary of that endangered language.

In 1998, John was nominated for the Alaska Governor's Award for his contributions to the preservation of Alaska Native languages and cultures. In 1999, Ahtna Traditional Chief Harry Johns held a special ceremony to designate John as a Traditional Ahtna Culture Bearer, a term usually reserved for elders with significant cultural knowledge. John Smelcer is the author of over fifty books, including *Beautiful Words: The Complete Ahtna Poems,* the only existing literature published in the Ahtna language. His award-winning novels include *The Trap, The Great Death, Edge of Nowhere, Lone Wolves, Savage Mountain, Stealing Indians* and *Kiska*. In 1995, John co-edited *Durable Breath: Contemporary Native American Poetry*. In 2013, with Joseph Bruchac (Abenaki), John co-edited *Native American Classics*, a graphic novel of 19th and early 20th century Native American literature. For almost a quarter century, John Smelcer served as poetry editor at *Rosebud*, making him one of the longest serving editors at a major magazine in American history. Aside from a Ph.D. in English and creative writing, John's education includes postdoctoral studies at Oxford, Cambridge, and Harvard. Dr. Smelcer is the inaugural writer-in-residence for the Charter for Compassion. Learn more at www.johnsmelcer.com